My First ZOO Animals

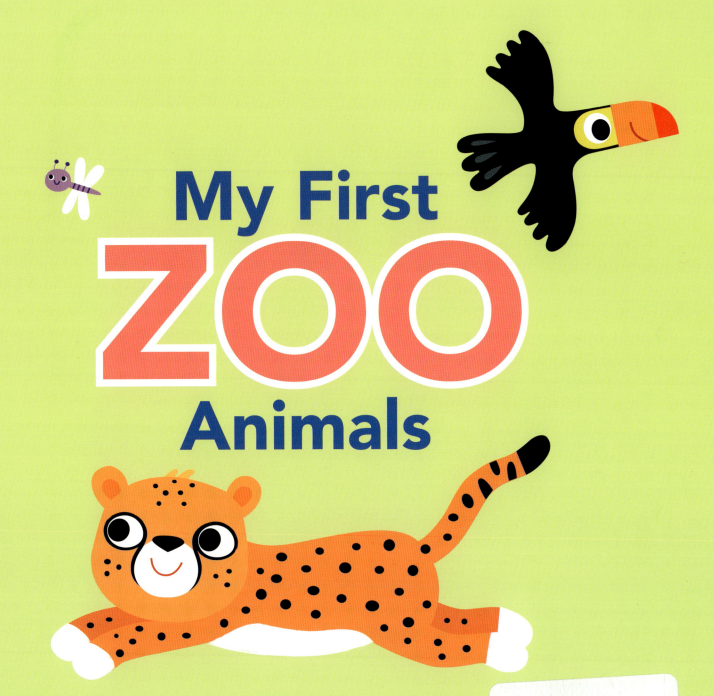

W. Books

Lions roar loudly and have beautiful manes.

Kangaroos jump high and love to play games.

Monkeys eat bananas and live in trees.

Giraffes have long necks and like to eat leaves.

Elephants are grey and grow big and tall.

Some snakes are long and some snakes are small!

Owls are nocturnal; they stay awake all night.

Toucans are tropical - watch them take flight!

Hippos love mud and bask on the shore.

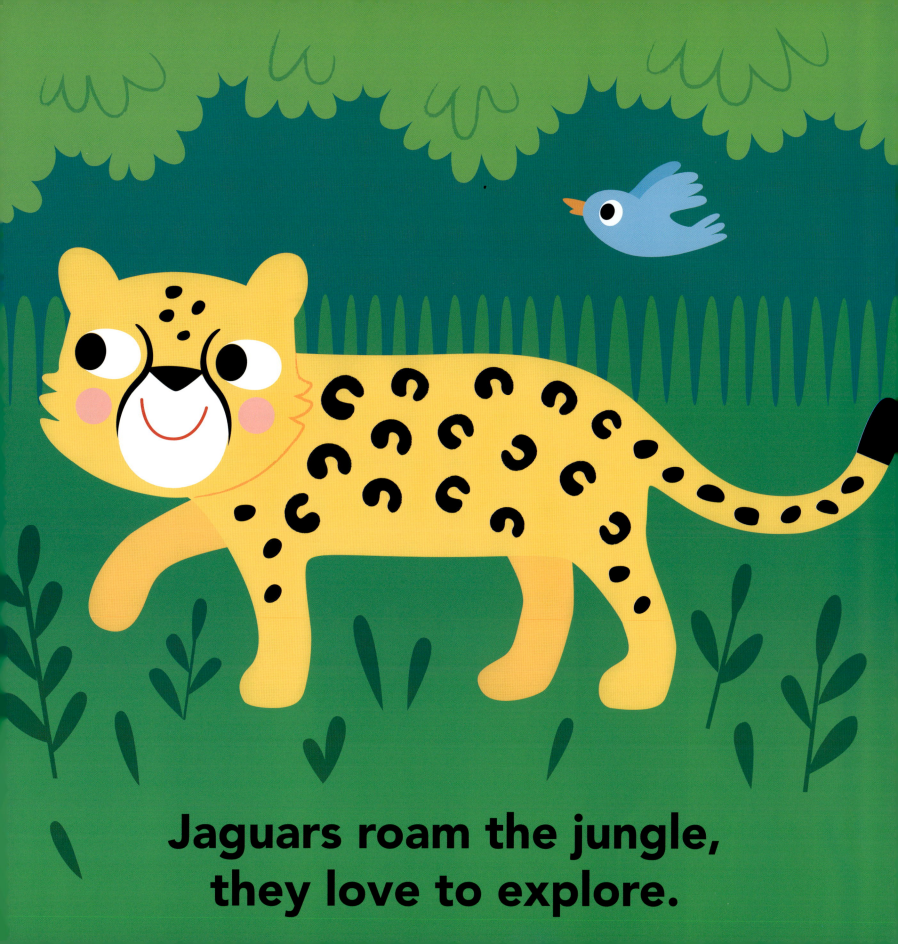

Jaguars roam the jungle, they love to explore.

Cheetahs are speedy, with spots on their back.

Polar bears live up North where there's lots of snow.

Penguins love dancing, just look at them go!

Alligators like sleeping on a big, sunny rock.

Frogs call out "RIBBIT" and go hippity-hop!

Zebras are graceful with beautiful stripes.

Otters hold hands with their friends while they sleep!

Koalas are cuddly and they love to play.